The Life and Times of Indigo Stone: 50 Life Lessons

By RL Collins

This is a work of fiction. All characters and events portrayed in this novel are fictitious or used fictitiously. All rights reserved. No part of this book may be reproduced in any form or by any electronic or mechanical means, including information storage and retrieval systems, without written permission from the publisher or author, except in the case of a reviewer, who may quote brief passages in review.

Indigo Stone, Publisher

The Life and Times of Indigo Stone: 50 Life Lessons

Copyright © 2020 by RL Collins

All Rights Reserved

Contents

PERSONAL 5

Beat COVID-19: Your Journal Prompt #101 6

Escape COVID-19 & Negative Self-Talk: Journal Prompt #102 8

Finding Gratitude During Crisis: Your Journal Prompt #103 11

Surviving COVID-19: Resume Tips 13

Releasing Fear Through Writing: Your Journal Prompt #104 15

Overcoming Obstacles: Resume Hacks 17

The Silver Lining: Your Journal Prompt #105 19

Grit vs. IQ: Your Journal Prompt #106 21

Self-Comparison Sucks: Your Journal Prompt #107 23

Drop the Grudge: Your Journal Prompt #108 25

Rebuilding the Fort: Your Journal Prompt #109 28

Embrace the Other: Your Journal Prompt #110 30

Role Model, Be One: Your Journal Prompt #111 32

Illusions: Your Journal Prompt #112 34

Love and Independence: Your Journal Prompt #113 36

Justice Without the Courts: Your Journal Prompt #114 38

Self-Reflection During the Pause: Your Journal Prompt #115 41

No More Crap: Your Writing Prompt #116 43

Hope and Action: Your Journal Prompt #117 45

Set Powerful Intentions: Your Journal Prompt #119 47

Love in the Valley: Your Journal Prompt #120 50

Love Letters During COVID-19 52

Day by Day Strength 55

Learn to Accept Peace 57

BUSINESS 59

How to Write Business Emails 60

How to Craft an Employee Evaluation Form - Part 1 62

How to Craft an Employee Evaluation Form – Part 2 64

Small Business Have Opportunities Through Grants 66

Always Consider the Audience in Business Writing 68

Strategies to Write for a Lay Audience 70

General Overview: How to Plan Your Writing 73

The First 5 Steps to Speech Writing 76

Steps to Speech Writing – Part 2 78

Where to Find Inspiration to Write 80

Early Tips to Better Writing 82

Early Tips to Better Writing – Part 2 84

How to Write a Holiday Thank You 86

How to Journal Your Thoughts 88

How to Write a Song 90

How to Write Personal Objectives 92

Happy New Year! Write that Resume – Part 1 94

New Year, New You! Write that Resume – Part 2 97

Write that Resume – Part 3, The Hook 99

Write that Resume – Part 4, The Meat 101

How to Write a Cover Letter – Dip a Toe into the Pool 103

How to Write a Cover Letter – Shining with Pizazz! 105

How to Write a Cover Letter – Avoid Common Pitfalls 107

Spring Forward, Spring into That New Job! 109

How to Write a Cover Letter – Getting Creative! 111

How to Write a Cover Letter – Bringing Home the Bacon 113

PERSONAL

1
Beat COVID-19: Your Journal Prompt #101

#StayTheFHome #QuarantineLife #SocialDistancing has many of us stressed out to the max! Journaling is a great tool to manage stress. Managing stress keeps difficult emotions from escalating into anxiety or depression. Use a journal to analyze emotions with the intent to cope with difficulties and challenges. Writing helps release tension. Writing helps understand the uncomfortable situations we may find ourselves in.

Stress management is great for the mind and body. Effective journaling may bring the following benefits:

1. Decrease some health symptoms
2. Strengthen the immune system
3. Improve cognitive function
4. Support goal-setting and positive action plans
5. Shift the mind into a more positive perspective
6. Reduce ruminating and over-thinking

Journaling your thoughts requires little resources. Frankly, all you need is pen and paper. If you have regular access to technology, you can use a mobile device, laptop, tablet, etc. Start today and release worries.

Journal Prompt #101:
Write about a time when work felt real, necessary, and/or satisfying. The work could be paid, unpaid, professional, domestic, or mental.

Use a journal to analyze emotions with the intent to cope with difficulties and challenges.

2

Escape COVID-19 & Negative Self-Talk: Journal Prompt #102

I can't do this anymore! I hate being inside! When is this over?! **Escape COVID-19 and minimize the negative self-talk through journaling.** Negative self-talk has many forms. At times, it may sound practical and other times it can sound downright mean.

Realistic: I'm not too good at this, I better watch my safety.

Mean: I can never do anything right!

Sometimes, self-talk is a grounded appraisal of our abilities. Other times, small doubts can explode into fear-based fantasies.

Grounded: I just got a "C" on this test. History might not be my best subject.

Fear-based Fantasy: I'll probably fail this History class and never get into college.

Basically, negative self-talk is an inner dialogue that may be limiting your ability to believe in yourself, acknowledge strengths, and reach your potential.

During this time of COVID-19, we are all doing the best we can. Don't beat yourself up if you are struggling emotionally or mentally. Different people handle crisis in different ways. Journal writing is a great way to minimize negative self-talk.

Writing about personal thoughts and feelings is a self-care tool. You can avoid putting additional pressure or fear on your loved ones by taking private moments to vent on paper. Be your own hero. Writing can positively impact your anxiety through:

- Calming and clearing your mind
- Releasing pent-up feelings and everyday stress
- Letting go of negative thoughts
- Exploring your experiences with anxiety
- Writing about your struggles and your successes

Do not wait for the perfect moment to start writing. Grab a pen and piece of paper. Grab your laptop or tablet. Here is this week's journal prompt:

Describe in detail a compassionate way you've supported a family member or friend. Then write down how you can do the same for yourself.

Escape COVID-19 and minimize the negative self-talk through journaling.

3

Finding Gratitude During Crisis: Your Journal Prompt #103

Practicing gratitude is an extremely effective tool for coping during a crisis. Regularly expressing thankfulness also helps you ride the peaks and valleys in life. There are different ways to express feeling blessed. Gratitude journaling will deliver most if not all the benefits.

The dictionary definition of gratitude states: "the quality of being thankful; readiness to show appreciation for and to return kindness." Simply put, whether you are having a good day or bad day, you find a few things to appreciate in your life. You can be thankful that you woke up in good health when others may be struggling. You can be thankful for having food in the refrigerator when others do without. You can be grateful for having access to family through technology when others live in a drop zone.

Journaling every day is a great habit to start. Expressing gratitude through writing has a wealth of benefits. For example, you may experience the following:

1. Boost your long-term well-being, encouraging exercise, reducing physical pain and symptoms, and increasing both length and quality of sleep
2. Increase your optimism and, indirectly, your happiness and health
3. Make you friendlier, more open, and expand your social support network
4. Help you make progress toward your goals

Gratitude journaling requires little resources. There are free mobile apps where you can log your daily appreciation. Every day pick three things you are grateful for – no matter how large or small. Express what you are grateful for and the "because." Adding the why is important and sparks your "feel good" brain center.

Are you ready to try it? Here we go…

Journal Prompt #103: What is a popular song that you enjoy? And why do you like it?

Regularly expressing thankfulness also helps you ride the peaks and valleys in life.

4
Surviving COVID-19: Resume Tips

When will life goes back to normal after COVID-19? What have you done during the wait? When companies open their doors, you need to step up with your resume.

Employers only spend 10 seconds glancing at a resume. You need to grab their attention and pull them in with a great resume. Do a little research to understand your industry. Look at what has been done in the past, then punch it up with a few key words that make you stand out.

Research your ideal job. It is important to tailor your summary to the job. Search for your ideal positions. Then, compile a list of common job requirements and preferred qualifications.

Assess your qualifications. How do you measure up? Be confident, but humble. You do not have to match every aspect of the job vacancy, 100%. But you do not want to land the job and require basic training on your day-to-day responsibilities. Outside of the minimum requirements, can you describe bonus skills you bring to the table? Also, if you are lacking in one area, how can you make up for in another area? Remember to clearly relay how you would benefit to the company.

Choose a headline strategy. Your resume title should be concise. Consider using bold, italics, or capitalized letters. But remain conservative and professional. Avoid bright colors and font better suited for arts and crafts projects. If you have space for a sub-heading, this is the place to add your personal stamp. Refer to an accomplishment or skill that helped you rock it in a previous project or position. Also remember to tailor the headline to the industry you want to be in.

Use a career objective. Do not literally label the career objective as an "objective" in the resume. The content of your objective should be woven into your career summary. The objective should send the message of – *this is who I am as a professional, competent employee.* Avoid the giving the impression – *this is who I want to be in the future.* The objective should show your benefit to the company. Remember to be concise and specific.

You do not have to match every aspect of the job vacancy, 100%. But you do not want to land the job and require basic training on your day-to-day responsibilities.

5

Releasing Fear Through Writing: Your Journal Prompt #104

We are living in trying times. It is normal to feel difficult emotions. There are different strategies for releasing fear in a way that is healthy and positive. Believe in the power of the pen. Write!

Recognize the sense of fear. After a certain point in life, many of us never say out loud that we are afraid. We are used to children expressing difficult feelings after having a nightmare, seeing a big spider, or watching a scary movie. Adults typically ignore it, bury it, or run from it. Accept that things happen in life outside of our control. It can be scary as hell.

Look at the history of your fear. You can write this down. Ask yourself: *Have I ever felt this fear before? How do I really feel (mentally and/or physical)? What am I actually afraid of? Loss? Disappointment? Being Alone?*

Fear creates opportunity. When you feel difficult emotions, it can be hard to see it as an opportunity. Feeling fear is not a fun experience. However, every struggle we have in life is an opportunity to come out stronger and braver:

Journaling is a great way to express and release fear. Writing is limitless. There is no required word count for journaling. Writing has no judgement. Your journal is for your eyes only. Spouses, family, and friends do not need to read your journal. Writing can take any form. You can make up random words to suit your emotions. If you want to do an abstract doodle, that's fine too. Maybe you feel inspired to rhyme and write in song. When you journal, you are in charge.

Face the fear. Write it out. Release it. Once you put it to paper, you no longer need to ruminate. Stop the overthinking! Redirect your thoughts to finding a solution or positive next steps.

Here is journal prompt #104: *Make a list of 25 things that make you smile. Then snap a picture of your smile. Tuck it away in your journal. Put in on your bathroom mirror. Or if you are feeling bold, text it to a good friend and start a light conversation.*

After a certain point in life, many of us never say out loud that we are afraid.

6
Overcoming Obstacles: Resume Hacks

Help a prospective employer make a quick decision to call you by crafting a nice resume. The work history is the real "meat" to any resume.

Hiring Managers have a difficult task. They need to fill job vacancies, but they must wade through poorly written resumes. **Hack #1: Do not copy the job description.**

Hack #2: Boast your problem-solving skills. Describe challenges, actions to overcome challenges, and results of your efforts in your work experience. Before you write the work history, you might consider drafting a list of all accomplishments in the last 10 years. Add the most impressive accomplishments to the resume. Write the result of your efforts, before concisely describing the problem and action.

Hack #3: Make it readable. Use a combination of bullets and paragraphs in work histories to keep it readable but not monotonous. Hiring managers need to be able to rest their eyes. Clearly label accomplishments as "accomplishments" or "key contributions." Be concise. The resume should hook the reader and land you an interview. Do not tell your whole life story in a resume.

Hack #4: As always target the job vacancy. Use power words. You can find powerful verbs and synonyms online. Be honest. An honest and well-written resume will be called for interviews.

Universal Hack #5: Proofread, refine, and perfect. No matter how you tackle resume writing, you get one chance to make a first impression. Avoid simple errors. You need to check and double check the resume. Have a trusted friend proofread and check for tone.

No matter how you tackle resume writing, you get one chance to make a first impression.

7
The Silver Lining: Your Journal Prompt #105

Calm and clear your mind. Consider your struggles and successes. When you wake up in the morning do you choose to try again? Or just lay in bed defeated? If you choose to try again, that is the silver lining. Write it down. Hold on to it.

Keeping a journal can help you commit to seeing the positive side of life and set goals. Your ideas to overcome challenges may be fuzzy at first. However, the process of writing and rewriting can create a laser focus.

Try to set aside fifteen to twenty minutes a day to journal. Review your goals, think about your options to accomplish tasks, then prioritize. If possible, write around the same time each day.

Journaling allows you to record progress. If you have struggles or setbacks you can record it in your journal. Then you work through to solutions and see the silver lining. If you ever have a difficult day, you can take out your journal and review the progress you have made.

Writing is an opportunity to explore your feelings and address barriers to your progress. Sometimes we are our own worst enemy. We do not believe in ourselves. We let doubts hold us back. We have negative self-talk. Journal all the negative feelings. Release them. Then plan realistic next steps to achieving your important goals.

Finally, journaling can help you keep the ball rolling. Vent the difficult emotions. Identify the silver lining. Create a to do list. Each day before you close the journal, give yourself an assignment. Choose something you can accomplish in the next 24-48 hours.

Ready for this week's journal prompt?

Prompt #105: Make a list of everything that inspires or motivates you. It could range from books to quotes to art to grandparents even the sunrise. Pick one or two to tuck away in your journal, set as the wallpaper on your laptop, or post to social media for fun conversation.

Writing is an opportunity to explore your feelings and address barriers to your progress. Sometimes we are our own worst enemy.

8
Grit vs. IQ: Your Journal Prompt #106

I think I can. I think I can. Grit.

To be successful in this world, you need more than just IQ points. Grit, the ability to persevere, will carry you through the darkest times.

Grit is not really taught in schools today. If you struggle in school, you get a low grade, then you move on to the next lessons. You may or may not get the chance to improve. You may or may not even understand *how* you are missing the mark.

Real grit and determination mean you take a hard look at what is not working, diagnose the problem, then take steps to correct it. The correction may happen in a few minutes, few days, or few months. But you keep at it until you get it.

Times today are difficult. Some of us may have adequate support from family, friends, or local agencies. And some of us may not. Dig deep. Look honestly at your challenges. What steps can you take to self-correct?

If you cannot pay the rent or mortgage and a local agency has not come through, what else can you do? Some industries are booming during this crisis. Grab your face mask and gloves and deliver groceries to those who need it. Walk the pets of owners who are too afraid to go out. Care for the children of moms and dads on the frontlines.

In many ways, we are dealing with much loss and stagnation. But through grit and determination, there are also opportunities to dig deep and survive. If you are not sure where to begin—grab your journal and brainstorm. First, vent your fears, worries, and frustrations. Get it all off your chest. Then, list possible solutions. Google it if you need to. Dream big. Start small.

Here is your journal prompt for this week:

If you could go back in time and talk to yourself at 12, what is the one thing you would say?

Grit, the ability to persevere, will carry you through the darkest times.

9

Self-Comparison Sucks: Your Journal Prompt #107

Comparing yourself to other people is a great way to make yourself feel terrible. Stop doing it!

Before COVID-19, our self-comparison may have centered around wealth, status, and beauty. Now, we struggle with our partners, family, and friends trying to decide who is more miserable. Understand this – everybody has a sad story.

Everybody has struggled privately or publicly. There is no hierarchy. When you compare yourself to someone and feel inferior, that really sucks. When you compare yourself to someone and feel superior, you are alone at the top. Today, we can all make a choice to grow.

Self-love and self-respect are an antidote. We don't need to have internal competition with the people around us. When you are happy with #1, you don't need to overanalyze what other people are doing in their lives.

Redirect your self-talk and outward expression. Give words of encouragement to someone you see is struggling. Say thank you for small acts of kindness. Show empathy to someone expressing difficult emotions.

In different parts of our nation, COVID-19 restrictions are gradually being lifted. Step outside into the sun. Bring someone special with you. It is okay to smile and feel a sense of renewed freedom.

Grab your laptop, notepad, or phone to record the progress you have made. Here is this week's journal prompt:

What is unconditional love? How does it look or feel to you?

When you compare yourself to someone and feel inferior, that really sucks. When you compare yourself to someone and feel superior, you are alone at the top.

10

Drop the Grudge: Your Journal Prompt #108

We all make mistakes. Sometimes we need to give forgiveness. Sometimes we need to receive forgiveness.

Holding on to grudges because of perceived wrongs can make us sick mentally or physically. At times, hurt is part of life. A parent may criticize us. A partner may cheat. That co-worker might steal your best project idea. We have no real control over the behavior of other people. However, we do have control over our reactions.

It is easy to hold a grudge. Some people are naturally more grudge-holding than others. We also feel more anger and resentment when we love or trust the person who betrays us. To reach a state of forgiveness you may have to work at it.

Real forgiveness is letting go of the resentment and need for revenge against another person.

You might always remember the hurtful action, but forgiveness releases you from being under someone else's control. It is not an excuse for the betrayal. Forgiveness is the path to more peace, stability, and joy in life.

Journaling is a great way to develop forgiveness for ourselves and those around us. You can write a letter to the person in your journal. In the letter, you tell it like it is. Explain very clearly what hurt you and how you feel about it. Vent everything you want to receive to feel better. Get it off your chest. If you can communicate with the person who betrayed you, the letter can be talking points to resolve the conflict.

If you are the one who needs to receive forgiveness, you can write down your thoughts and feelings about what you did and why. When you write, explain all the messy details of your actions. No one will see it. You can come back to the journal as often as you need to. Hopefully, one day you can go to the person you offended and give a genuine apology. However, be mindful, that just because you give an apology, the other person may not "hear it" or accept it. But you will have done your best to reconcile.

Use this week's journal prompt to reflect on the need to let go of grudges. In life, there are misunderstandings— large and small.

Prompt #108: In your opinion, how would forgiveness change world politics?

Real forgiveness is letting go of the resentment and need for revenge against another person.

11
Rebuilding the Fort: Your Journal Prompt #109

Sometimes life smacks you in the face. You didn't even see it coming. Maybe you are blindsided by a job loss. Maybe you are surprised by the passing of a loved one. Maybe you are used to a certain way of doing things, then the rules change. The world can be unpredictable.

After you roll through the anger, grief, and uncertainty – you have a decision to make. Stay stuck or rebuild? Choosing to rebuild your life, heart, or mind is the mark of maturity. You can rebuild stronger and wiser. You may even reach a point where the past is simply a lesson learned.

Writing can help you process difficult situations. Through journaling you can be brutally honest. You can write and write, until there is no more to say. Then you start to plan for a better future. Use the journal to set goals, timeframes, and problem solve. Be your own cheerleader during the reconstruction.

Keeping a journal is easy and inexpensive. It never gets tired of listening to you. You can be as silly or angry as you want. You can brainstorm plans and ideas until you are ready to make them reality. Set aside a few minutes each day to write. It is for your eyes only.

Here is this week's journal prompt #109:

In life, there are rarely second chances. If you had one "do over" what would it be and why?

Choosing to rebuild your life, heart, or mind is the mark of maturity. You can rebuild stronger and wiser

12

Embrace the Other: Your Journal Prompt #110

His skin color is different than mine. Her eyes are different. Look at that hair, those clothes, the walk. They are all from *over* there!

Too many of us see healthy differences and judge them as inferior or something to be afraid of. Movies, books, and other entertainment remake the "Other" and turn it into a villain. The bad guys wear hoodies and listen to rap music. Someone new in the neighborhood might be up to no good and a thief. People who voice opposing opinions might turn violent and do us harm.

This is all nonsense. We exaggerate the differences in our personalities, communities, and cultures to inspire hate. Some people with no other sense of spirit and life can band together in hate.

Wise up. The "Other" is what makes life interesting. We can separate plasma from blood because of the "Other." We can analyze galaxies with an x-ray spectrometer because of the "Other." We found the precursor to dry cleaning because of the "Other." Children play with the super soaker water toy, because of the "Other." Dark purple berry lipstick exists because of the creativity of the "Other."

Use this week's journal prompt to celebrate differences in form, thought, and life.

Prompt #110: Describe a time when you stepped outside your comfort zone. How did it make you feel? What did you learn? Who did you meet along the way?

Wise up. The "Other" is what makes life interesting. We can separate plasma from blood because of the "Other."

13

Role Model, Be One: Your Journal Prompt #111

In the world, we are slowly recovering from a pandemic. In the USA, we are exploring reform to stop racial injustice. Everybody has an opinion on how to bring about change. March here. Donate there. Tweet that.

Be a ROLE MODEL. If you care about your community and want to stop the spread of COVID-19, wear a mask every time. If you believe in racial equality, do not flinch when a person of color doesn't smile through an offense. Sit down. Listen. Hear what he/she has to say.

Do what you can as you can. It does not really require you to spend to spend money if you don't have the finances. It doesn't require you to step out in the streets if you have children or vulnerable family at home. Do not minimize the need for revolution down to a social media tweet or post.

Start SMALL. Get really clear about what you believe. Explore your faith, values, and desires for the kind of nation you want to live in. Write it down! Use a journal to address every issue in your community that bothers you.

Next, outline a vision of that hero beating the challenges. What would this person do every day, every week, and every month? Do not edit yourself. Get it all down on paper. Now you need to realize, YOU are that hero. You are the person that can take a stand in large and small ways.

If you see an injustice, speak on it, write about it, go to the other person, and ask, "Are you okay?" If you see someone bullied in the workplace, do not join in, don't turn a blind eye. Behind the scenes, maybe you help that person proofread an important memo. Maybe you invite your neighbor over for dinner, who has just lost his job.

The options are endless. It is up to you. This is how we ALL take a stand. Use this week's journal prompt to find your inner hero.

Journal Prompt #111: Use your imagination to draft a recipe for peace as you see it. What are the "ingredients," cooking tools, and directions for serving a group?

Be a ROLE MODEL. If you believe in racial equality, do not flinch when a person of color doesn't smile through an offense.

14

Illusions: Your Journal Prompt #112

There is perception and there is truth. We often write grand "stories" about ourselves and the people around us—to be retold repeatedly in our minds. The stories often skew towards the negative. Our ancestors survived with a grand sense of pessimism towards the unknown or one bad experience. *Don't eat those purple berries, they might make you sick!*

Nowadays, we often develop fantasies when dealing with other people. In these illusions, we are quick to make ourselves the hero and the stranger a villain. Sometimes, just sometimes, there is *nothing* there. Outside the lives of celebrities, gurus, and world leaders, we are mostly ordinary people. We have our good days. We have bad days. Life is a series of peaks and valleys.

Perception is how we *choose* to see things. Perception cannot be proven true or not true. It is what makes the most sense to us. We feel very comfortable with an idea even when it inspires difficult emotions.

Dropping the illusion and seeing the truth of a matter, can be challenging. Truth can be ordinary. Truth can be strange. Truth can be funny. When it feels impossible to find the truth, or you simply do not have the *detective* tools, walk away. Harsh words are not needed. Wild accusations are not needed. Do not feel a need to rally the troops (friends) and get everybody on your side. Just walk away. Let go of the need to be right. Hang on to the reality that we are all plodding along looking for a happiness that can be defined in 101 ways.

Here is this week's journal prompt #112:

The last time I laughed, was _____ .

In these illusions, we are quick to make ourselves the hero and the stranger a villain. Sometimes, just sometimes, there is *nothing* there.

15

Love and Independence: Your Journal Prompt #113

He loves me. He loves me not. She loves me. She loves me not.

Love of self eliminates the need to be approved and accepted by others. You can just BE.

What is self-love? When you love yourself, you accept your strengths and weakness. You can always strive to be better, but perfection is an illusion. Sometimes all hell breaks loose, and things get messy. But that is part of life. You laugh it off. You cry and get tissue. You get mad and scream in your car. But then you bounce back and keep at it.

Having love of self, also means you understand that the world does not owe you anything. It is not another person's responsibility to make you happy or entertain you. Do not expect someone to make radical changes to accommodate you and your desires. You have the power obtain your own happiness.

How do you develop self-love? At some point, you take a hard look at who you are in life. What makes you strong? What makes you falter? Then balance the line between what is healthy and excessive. Setting boundaries around difficult people and difficult situations is important. Some challenges in life are necessary, but if a person or situation regularly upsets you, cut them out.

Create the opportunity for daily pleasures. You can love dark chocolate and have a bite after dinner. But you might not want to eat a whole bar, every day, indefinitely. Try the decadent hand cream that comes in the tiny jar. You might not use it every day, all day long, but maybe slather it on before bed. See the sunrise on a Sunday morning. However, it may not be something you can commit to every day with work, family, etc. Start small, carve out the time, enjoy daily pleasures.

Ready to write? Here is your journal prompt #113: *Make a list of 25 activities you love, want more of, and look forward to it. This is your "menu" of daily pleasures. Everything in moderation.*

Having love of self, also means you understand that the world does not owe you anything.

16
Justice Without the Courts: Your Journal Prompt #114

Have you ever felt the sting of injustice? This week's blog post has real-world secrets for navigating unethical people and situations. After reading this post, please use your power of persuasion for good, not evil.

"The world is an ugly place." You have probably heard this before. We can all see the TV ads for lawsuits against talcum powder cancer, childbirth mishaps, and car accidents. Everybody wants to sue. Everybody wants justice. I am a VICTIM!

If there has been no real physical or financial injury, you do NOT have a court case. The best justice is prevention, reading early warning signs, and DISCRETION. Never tell someone who is ugly to you, that they are ugly. The person will work that much harder to be petty and throw down unnecessary obstacles.

When faced with the devil, kill her with kindness. Discreetly navigate around predatory people.

If you get a sloppy meal in a restaurant, do not complain to the waiter. Do not give them time to prepare another meal with a side of spit. Smile and say, "no thanks." Try another restaurant. If you have a backstabbing coworker stealing your best ideas, change how you share your ideas. Instead of brainstorming with individuals, keep it to yourself, polish it, then share in team meetings. Put the grand idea in writing. If you are looking to buy a property, you have proven written qualifications, and there is real estate discrimination – do not waste your time getting a lawyer. Larger companies know the laws better than you. Take your case to the consumer alert department of your local news station. Most businesses hate bad publicity and will work with you to resolve the issue privately.

Use your power of persuasion for good, not evil. Do not complain about people and systems because you are having a bad day, or your favorite TV show was canceled. There are supposed to be challenges in life that we grow through. But when faced with a real INJUSTICE—stand up for yourself, navigate around, and SMILE.

Here is this week's journal prompt:

Describe a time when you stood up for the underdog in your family, community, or workplace.

When faced with the devil, kill her with kindness. Discreetly navigate around predatory people.

17

Self-Reflection During the Pause: Your Journal Prompt #115

Stoplights. Thunderstorms. Pandemics. At times, life pauses, and we have the opportunity breathe in the moment. We can sit down for a bit and really look at our life. What is working? What is not working? What are our next steps?

Having time to self-reflect is a powerful gift. Most of us spend every waking minute of our lives on the go. We jump out of bed, grab a cup of coffee, and race to work. A friend calls us, we throw on our best outfit, and run to happy hour. Our family, friends, and coworkers need us.

Respect the pause. Whether your life is on hold by choice or by force—just sit down for a minute.

Real self-reflection is when you take an honest look at your life without judgment. There is no good or bad. You see where you have been, where you are now, and where you want to be in the future. It is an opportunity to silence the noise. Deep down how are YOU feeling? What do YOU want? How do YOU spend most of your time?

It can be difficult to hear our inner voice when we are constantly absorbing messages from different people and situations. Family says one thing. A partner may say something else. A favorite news station can deliver the opposite message. We can forget who we are and what is important to us in life.

At the next stoplight, check in with yourself. Ask yourself, what do I hope to achieve at my next destination? During the next thunderstorm, do a forgotten activity that brings you joy. If you are still on pause during the pandemic, grab your journal, and draft plan B for the next 3-6months.

Here is your writing prompt for this week: What is absolutely, necessary and what can I let go?

Respect the pause. Whether your life is on hold by choice or by force—just sit down for a minute.

18

No More Crap: Your Writing Prompt #116

Do you ever feel pulled in different directions? Your family wants this. Your job wants that. The kids are buzzing around needing this AND that. Sometimes, just sometimes, the stress and anxiety you feel in life has nothing to do with you. It is OTHER people's crap! Learn to drop it.

First sign of crap: Every time you are around a certain person or situation you feel tense. If you can wake up feeling good, then flip a switch when you meet a certain person—it is NOT you. The person you are dealing with has a certain energy. Maybe there was a previous incident. Maybe they communicate in a difficult manner. Find a mutual friend to help bring you two together. Or limit your time with this person if you cannot pinpoint the source of conflict.

Second sign of crap: Your stomach hurts. Some people are very stoic. They carry themselves through life. They carry whole tribes on their back and never say a word. If you find that your digestion is off every time you are in a certain situation, it is NOT you. The environment you are in is not healthy for you. Speak up. Ask for help. Or drop it and lighten your load.

Third sign of crap: You frequently get robbed in tangible and intangible ways. Sometimes you meet snake charmers. These are people who smile and are very charismatic. However, every time you around this person you lose something. You lose time. You lose money. You lose power. You find yourself saying yes to things you should not be doing. It is NOT you. You are dealing with someone who is great at manipulation. Run, run far away.

The best way to prevent getting sucked into other people's crap is to "know thy self." Know what you will and will not stand for. Learn to say no in diplomatic ways. Build healthy, personal boundaries. Set aside time to be alone and turn off the noise. When you are always around other people, you constantly take in their energy and opinions. It is good to sit in the silence and reconnect with yourself. You may do this through journaling, meditation, gaming, gardening, etc. Pick an activity you enjoy and can perform solo.

Here is journal prompt #116: The last time I sat in silence, I discovered...

Sometimes, just sometimes, the stress and anxiety you feel in life has nothing to do with you. It is OTHER people's crap! Learn to drop it.

19

Hope and Action: Your Journal Prompt #117

"Without action, you aren't going anywhere." Mahatma Gandhi

With hope you can survive anything. With hope and action, you do not just survive but you thrive. Hope is believing without seeing. Take your hope and persevere towards a goal through action. Even when you do not know all the steps and obstacles up ahead, take one step at a time.

Through journaling you can record daily motivational messages to keep your hope strong. Whether the nuggets of wisdom come from you, family, or unsung heroes – it does to matter. Write it down and let it seep into your soul. Then back it up with action.

The same journal can be used to make 30, 60, 90-day plans in career, family, personal growth, etc. The trick is that the journal is for your eyes only. It does not matter if you make little mistakes or are unsure about what you tell yourself. Keep it positive. Make little adjustments. Consistently work towards your goals. Let hope lull you to sleep. Allow action to wake you up full of passion and energy. Whether it takes you one week, one month, or one year – believe in yourself.

Here is your journal prompt for the week: My hope today is…
Tomorrow, my next step towards this wish, will be…

With hope and action, you do not just survive but you thrive.

20

Set Powerful Intentions: Your Journal Prompt #119

"Choose to be optimistic, it feels better." — *Dalai Lama*

Distractions. Did that cashier roll her eyes? I wanted that parking spot, now he has it. I hate waiting in line at DMV. There are tons of distractions in the world today that can throw you off track. The key to survival is to set positive intentions. Put on angelic blinders to ignore the small stuff and set a strong focus.

Normally, the idea of putting on blinders has a negative connotation. But in this context, you must do it! Family, friends, and co-workers are dealing with COVID-19, an uncertain economy, and other stressors you may or may not know about. Focus on YOU. Make sure you have your *sh*t* together. IGNORE small irritations that you cannot change.

If you are a night owl, set your daily intentions before you go to bed. If you are a morning person, set your daily intentions when you first wake up. Basically, all that matters during times of stress is maintaining food, shelter, clothing, and gas in your car or funds for public transportation. Take care of your own needs for survival first. When you are strong and stable, reach back and help others. You cannot help anybody if your "cup is empty.

Use this week's journal prompt #119 to help you get started:

There are limited hours in one day. Today, the top three things I must accomplish are...

This week, it is necessary that I accomplish the following tasks for peace and stability...

In the next 30 days, my household will be stronger if I satisfy these five goals...

Love in the Valley: Your Journal Prompt #120

Life by definition involves changes. Nothing last forever. Impermanence is a fact. When you find yourself in the valley, love yourself through it.

The real danger of being in the valley is believing there is no way out. There is a way out, it just might take time. The myth of being in the valley is thinking you are alone. Everybody finds themselves in the valley from time to time, they just might not tell you about it. The illusion of being in the valley is that it only happens one time. Once you accept that it is part of life, you embrace the highs, and remember the lessons to cope next time you are low.

What is love in the valley? Ask for help as you need it, whether it is family or a paid professional. Maintain healthy boundaries with others. If you are not up to that community event, do not go. Create positive routines around sleep, diet, and exercise. Everything is harder when you are tired, hungry, or achy. Venting difficult emotions is also love in the valley. You can journal, sing, garden, cook, make art – you decide whatever it is that makes you feel lighter.

Use this week's journal prompt to help you ride the highs and lows of life.

I love myself enough to make and keep this promise…

Today, I will set healthy boundaries by…

This week, I will reach out and talk to…

This month, I will set a plan for better sleep by…

The key to survival is to set positive intentions. Put on angelic blinders to ignore the small stuff and set a strong focus.

21
Love in the Valley: Your Journal Prompt #120

Life by definition involves changes. Nothing last forever. Impermanence is a fact. When you find yourself in the valley, love yourself through it.

The real danger of being in the valley is believing there is no way out. There is a way out, it just might take time. The myth of being in the valley is thinking you are alone. Everybody finds themselves in the valley from time to time, they just might not tell you about it. The illusion of being in the valley is that it only happens one time. Once you accept that it is part of life, you embrace the highs, and remember the lessons to cope next time you are low.

What is love in the valley? Ask for help as you need it, whether it is family or a paid professional. Maintain healthy boundaries with others. If you are not up to that community event, do not go. Create positive routines around sleep, diet, and exercise. Everything is harder when you are tired, hungry, or achy. Venting difficult emotions is also love in the valley. You can journal, sing, garden, cook, make art – you decide whatever it is that makes you feel lighter.

Use this week's journal prompt to help you ride the highs and lows of life.

I love myself enough to make and keep this promise…

Today, I will set healthy boundaries by…

This week, I will reach out and talk to…

This month, I will set a plan for better sleep by…

Everybody finds themselves in the valley from time to time, they just might not tell you about it.

22
Love Letters During COVID-19

"To write a good love letter, you ought to begin without knowing what you mean to say, and to finish without knowing what you have written." – Jean-Jacques Rousseau

It is believed that the act of writing can evoke feelings of love in the writer. A love letter has no formal rules around form, length, or style. You can write a love letter that is long, passionate, poetic—a real labor of love. You can write a love letter that is short with a few powerful words in a text. It is up to the writer to decide on the type of message to be communicated.

What is love? You can write about devotion, ambition, obsession, disappointment, forgiveness, etc. Love is many things to many people.

For You

We are living during uncertain times. Write a love letter to yourself of motivation, encouragement, and selfcare. Revel in the splendor of knowing who you are, what you stand for, and living your life as you see fit. Describe the freedom of being able to stand strong and imperfect during difficult times.

For Your Partner

You may be at a distance from your partner. Or you may be too close in quarantine with your partner. Write a love letter of forgiveness, commitment, and fantasy. Remember better times and make plans for an exciting future. Write a romantic scene for a world without corona and share it with your loved one.

For Your Family and Friends

All love does not have to be romantic. We can love our family. We can love our friends. Love is listening with our ears and our hearts. Love is making the effort to understand the other person. Write love and support notes to friends who may be unemployed or furloughed. Write loving words to family who may sick and in recovery. Create a word collage of love for children going back to school who may be nervous about a different kind of school year.

As the world spins, we need more love and kindness.

It is believed that the act of writing can evoke feelings of love in the writer.

23

Day by Day Strength

"With the new day comes new strength and new thoughts." -Eleanor Roosevelt

What is happening next week? Next month? Next year? Sometimes, we worry and obsess so much about the future, we forget today is here. Today is…HERE. Day by day strength means being grounded in the present and planting seeds for the future.

The best of us might have long-range plans, vision boards, to do list, and a marked-up calendar. But nothing happens without small steady steps towards progress. Whether your goal is to be a fitter you, Rockstar employee, or more organized parent – take it day by day.

We are summation of our daily habits. There is no guarantee of a tomorrow, next month, or next season. We have no immediate control over the weather, pandemics, international economies as ordinary citizens. Work with what you have. Write down daily goals. Leave room for missteps and those moments where we just "don't feel like it."

At times we feel like we must carry the weight of the world on our shoulders. But you just need to carry yourself through this moment. What is necessary in this moment? Do you have what you need to happy and whole in this moment? Are the people you love safe and well fed?

Whenever you come upon this post, stop for a moment, take a deep breath, and look around. Today is…HERE. What can you accomplish in this moment, without too much fuss?

Today is…HERE. What can you accomplish in this moment, without too much fuss?

24
Learn to Accept Peace

There may be uncertainty in our communities, the nation, and the world. But there are still opportunities to have peace. Fall has arrived giving us crisp mornings for walking a dog. Retailers are gearing up for the holidays cutting fabulous deals. Pumpkins and pumpkin spice lattes are back on the menu. *Write!*

Take the time to relax, relate, and release! Grab a journal or your phone to express your gratitude for moments of contentment and joy. All you must do is jot down a few words. "I am grateful for… because." Refill your bucket with selfcare and selflove. Write and breathe through it.

There are several benefits to writing:

- *It lowers stress and anxiety*
- *It helps you work through problem-solving*
- *It inspires creativity and can shift of perspective*
- *It keeps you mentally sharp as you mature*
- *It promotes life-long learning*

Accept that peace can be as simple as grabbing a piece of paper and writing in free verse *or* expressing the love of coffee in a gratitude app on your phone. It is inexpensive. It can be done 24/7. You can choose to be online or offline.

Grab a journal or your phone to express your gratitude for moments of contentment and joy.

BUSINESS

25
How to Write Business Emails

Emails. We all use them in the business world. Some use is appropriate. Some use is inappropriate. The purpose of a business email should be to convey basic information – no more. Tell your reader the "when, where, and how" of a business matter. Emails should not be sent in times of high emotion. Emails should not be drafted with sarcasm or off-color jokes. Professional emails should not be used as the first step to address a problem or concern with a colleague.

The culture of your organization and the relationship you have with the reader determines how formal your beginning and ending should be. For example, in a formal environment you may begin with the traditional, "Dear Mr./Ms." and the person's last name. A more relaxed, but still professional approach might be "Good Morning/Afternoon" and the receiver's first name. Whatever you do, never resort to texting style language in a business email, such as "Hey U." It is helpful to end an email with a call to action, highlighting next steps, or a simple "thank you" for the reader's attention.

It is also important to use clear and direct language in all business emails. This is especially important if you are communicating with different regions in your country or on the international platform. Different cultures interpret certain word choices differently. For example, if you use the slang "what's shaking?" to be friendly, this might be misinterpreted by someone with a different background. Use the standard, "how are you?" Whenever you write a business email, keep it simple, to the point, and free of typos.

Whenever you write a business email, keep it simple, to the point, and free of typos.

26
How to Craft an Employee Evaluation Form - Part 1

As a business leader or employer, it is critical to give employees constructive written feedback that supports professional growth and productivity within the organization. Everyone does not know how to give meaningful feedback. Everyone does not know how to accept meaningful feedback. The key is to have an evaluation system that is transparent, fair, and realistic.

An employee evaluation form should assess performance within 3-5 categories that are important to the short-term and long-term success of the business. The following are a few suggestions for developing top performance within staff:

- Success within a Team
- Success with Independent Tasks
- Oral and Written Communication
- Measurable Results and/or Accuracy of Work
- Ethics and/or Professionalism

The written criteria for each category should be brief, positive and have a few examples of the desired behavior.

Success within a Team: The employee makes tangible and intangible positive contributions to the team. The employee can navigate different viewpoints. The team can make meaningful progress towards goals and tasks with this employee. Examples of desired behavior include but are not limited to 1.) Having a pleasant demeanor 2.) Offering suggestions and feedback during discussions 3.) Has good time and attendance to team meetings.

The rating system for the evaluation form should range from unacceptable/needs improvement to exceeds expectations/excellent. It is also wise to pair the rating system with the use of points or a number scale (1-5). The form should help the supervisor and employee quantify performance, measure growth, and foster meaningful conversation.

The key is to have an evaluation system that is transparent, fair, and realistic.

27
How to Craft an Employee Evaluation Form – Part 2

All evaluation forms should be signed by the supervisor and employee with loose contractual language. In some organizations, the human resource lead, or a top executive such as the chief executive officer also sign the form. It is important to have checks and balances. No one should be working in a vacuum.

The contractual portion of the signature line should simply acknowledge that all the parties involved have discussed the contents of the evaluation and had the opportunity to ask questions. Do not require an employee to sign as an agreement or approval of the feedback. It is difficult for many people to receive constructive feedback. Some will disagree only because it is part of their nature. See the example below.

I have had the opportunity to review and discuss the contents of this evaluation with my supervisor and/or human resource lead. I do not agree or disagree with the contents.

Print Name (Employee):

Signature (Employee):

It is difficult for many people to receive constructive feedback. Some will disagree only because it is part of their nature.

28
Small Business Have Opportunities Through Grants

If you are a small business that needs start-up funding or financial support for a special project, consider grants. Specifically, if you are woman- or minority-owned. There are great ways to find available opportunities: 1.) Check with local government agencies 2.) Check with federal agencies 3.) Check with major corporations 4.) Search the internet 5.) Ask around locally 6.) Visit the local library for grant books and directories.

Important Tips for Grant Writing

The business of securing a federal, state, or private grant is competitive. The organization must craft a beautifully written, concise proposal that leaves *no room* for questions or doubts for the reader. The first thing to do before writing a grant proposal is to read the announcement multiple times. Make sure all requirements are understood. Then have a conversation with the team to double check that the organization is equipped to satisfy all requirements. Not most, but all. The team should also discuss if the award is worth the effort and inspires *full* commitment.

Consider the financial structure of the business. Can the organization handle the financial reporting requirements and related tasks? Finally, it must be decided who will write the grant proposal. Will the business use someone in-house or hire a professional grant writer? Regardless who does the writing, good proposals must include the following parts:

- Goals & Objectives
- Need
- Response
- Evaluation
- Impact
- Resources & Capabilities
- Budget

The organization must craft a professionally written, concise proposal that leaves *no room* for questions or doubts for the reader.

29
Always Consider the Audience in Business Writing

Regardless of the industry, consider the audience in all business writing. What is the purpose of the writing piece? What questions are to be answered? For example, when writing as an expert, information must be in a clear step-by-step order with potential precautions clearly presented. At times, expert writing benefits from visuals and diagrams. It is also valuable to offer resources for additional help.

When the audience is decision makers in business, time is money. Immediately present the request in writing. Decision makers have multiple demands on their time. The writing should be persuasive, articulate the benefit, and show that the writer can deliver a quality product.

Information published for the internet has a different set of expectations. Material on the internet is more likely to be skimmed rather than read word for word. Summarize key points at the top of the browser window. Use visuals, animations, audio clips, video clips to highlight key points. Chunk the text into bite size pieces.

There are a few things to consider when determining the needs of an audience:

- Who is the primary audience?
- Does the writing have multiple audiences?
- How knowledgeable are the primary and secondary audiences about the topic?
- Does the writing attempt to inspire or support an emotion (informative, motivational, stress relief, grief, etc.)?

When the audience is decision makers in business, time is money.

30
Strategies to Write for a Lay Audience

Take a pause—the world today has a short attention span. The average person will invest two minutes or less listening to a sound bite. The lay person will read about 140 written characters before deciding to stay or bounce. Explaining technical material is a challenge. How can it be done?

Be Concise

If the writer cannot explain it, he or she does not understand the material.

Improvise

If the audience gives feedback that the material is difficult to understand—revise, edit, restate the bottom line in a different way.

Tell Stories

Engineers and scientists often begin reports with data and statistics. This can be too dry for the lay audience. The movie trilogy, Lord of the Rings, can be a great story to build a case of increasing environmental protections. In Lord of the Rings, we have Bilbo Baggins on a journey to save the shire from ultimate evil while rallying support and battling self-doubt. Today, we live in a world where we have the numbers to prove the decline of our air, soil, and water. We need to rally together and lay down effective conservationism to battle the ultimate greed encouraging misuse of Mother Earth.

Use Visuals

Adding pictures to technical material, help the reader visualize summaries, reports, maps, timelines, etc. Visuals allow the material to appeal to a wider range of learning styles.

Use Analogies and Metaphors

Analogies and metaphors make technical information more relatable. Interventional radiology, micro-surgery through blood vessels in the human body, is to medicine what ordering home delivery for groceries is to busy families. Less fuss. Less muss.

Always Ask "So What?"

Finally, the lay audience wants to know the bottom line when reading technical material. So what? Why does this matter to me? The writer needs to clearly convey the practical day-to-day benefits of the technical piece.

The lay person will read about 140 written characters before deciding to stay or bounce.

31

General Overview: How to Plan Your Writing

To conquer oneself is a greater victory than to conquer thousands in a battle. – Dali Lama

We all have those moments of inspiration that need to be released. We grab the laptop or a mobile device and start to write…. then we stop. How am I going to do this? Will it be good enough? Planning your writing, is the first step to sharing your insights with the world.

Read Similar Authors

Before you start outlining, it is important to do some research. Read authors who have written about your topic. You need options to approach the topic from a different angle. Takes notes as you read. Note your sources (e.g. URLs, magazines, bibliographies, etc.). Keep your research organized in one place.

Develop Your Objective

Once you decide on the angle for your writing, write down the objective. What do you want readers to understand by the end? Write the objective in one sentence. Everything in the body of your written work should support the objective. The objective will help you focus and not wander off topic.

Do a Brain Dump

Once you have your topic and objective, do a "brain dump." Jot down all main points that come to mind. Do not worry about spelling, grammar, or punctuation. Write until you cannot write anymore. Save the information in one place with your earlier research.

Revise and Refine

After the brain dump, you need to decide the structure of your writing project. Will the content work well as a narrative? Expository writing? Persuasive? Or something else?

Review the points you have jotted down and cut everything that does not fit the topic. You may also find points that do not exactly fit but may be used as a sidebar. Put your ideas into a standard format. Do not be too formal. You may organize everything into bullets or a numbered list. All you need is enough information to remember where you are going, stay on track, and be organized.

Once you have your topic and objective, do a "brain dump."

32

The First 5 Steps to Speech Writing

"I've learned that people will forget what you said, people will forget what you did, but people will never forget how you made them feel."

-Maya Angelou

In writing a speech, you have two main objectives: Making a good impression and leaving your audience with one or two call-to-actions. The rest is just entertainment.

Make an Impression

Most people will only remember a line or two from your speech. Condense your message into 15-20 words and build the speech around it. There are different techniques to use. Using metaphors, analogies, surprise, and axioms are options that may be used.

Structure is Key

The audience expects two things from a speaker: A path and a destination. Set expectations in the beginning. As you write and revise the speech, keep it simple. Remove any confusing phrasing. If the text does not help the core message – drop it.

Make the Opening Shine

Share a shocking fact or statistic. Tell a humorous story related to the theme. Open with a question. Poll the audience so they must raise their hands. Make it count. Every minute you talk, you are losing the audience.

Use the Right Tone

Who is the audience? Why are they there? What do they want? You must answer all these questions before you write the speech. Decide whether the speech will inform, motivate, entertain, challenge or something else.

Make it Personal

Share a story about yourself. Throw in references to your family and/or community. Write like you are talking to a friend. You need to be yourself, your *best* self on stage.

The audience expects two things from a speaker:
A path and a destination.

33

Steps to Speech Writing – Part 2

Welcome to the second installment sharing steps to speech writing. Whether you are presenting at the office, at school, or for a civic organization – there are key points to remember.

Repeat Yourself

People have short attention spans. Condense your message into a few key points and repeat them throughout your presentation. Always look for places to tie the speech back to the main topic. Keep reinforcing your bottom line.

Use Transitions

Flag important messages with a good transition. Be direct if needed. You can say, "Here is the lesson." Use rhetorical questions, "What does this mean?" A dramatic pause will get people's attention.

Visuals Help

Using visuals during your speech will hammer in the message. You may choose props, demonstrations, videos, or even some dramatic interpretation. Keep it simple. Do not be afraid to use everyday items. Be bold. You want to be memorable.

End Strong

People will remember how you end the speech more than anything else. Recap your biggest takeaway. Tie everything together. Share a success story. Present a call to action. Stand strong. The ending is what the audience will share with their friends and family.

Be Concise

Less is more. Make your points and sit down. The longer you talk, people's minds will wander. The longer you talk, you might make mistakes. You are there to serve the audience.

Less is more. Make your points and sit down. The longer you talk, people's minds will wander.

34

Where to Find Inspiration to Write

Inspiration.

What is it? Where do we find it?

Most of the time we are given a writing assignment as part of a mundane project or to accomplish a goal. Perhaps the boss needs you to draft a PowerPoint presentation. Perhaps an instructor requires you to write an essay. Maybe you are opening for a civic event in your neighborhood. It is the heart and personality we inject into our writing that makes it come alive.

Brainstorm. Inspiration can be found in the sunset. Inspiration can be found in a 90's tune on YouTube. Hot coffee on a chilly afternoon can bring good feelings. Feel what you feel and write down the words and phrases that come to mind. Do not worry about spelling, grammar, or punctuation. Then pick the best tidbits to build your story.

Read the works of other writers. Lighten the mood and read a comic strip in the newspaper. Explore and read an article from a new magazine. Or if you really have the time, check out a book on short stories from the local library. There is no magic formula. Do not try too hard.

Review examples of art. Works of art can be found online and offline. If you are lucky, you might have art galleries or museums in your community. There are online marketplaces where you can browse art for inspiration. You may even try a happy hour painting session after work. There are options to suit one's taste.

In the end, give yourself time. There is no right or wrong method to finding inspiration to write. Satisfy the requirements for the writing assignment. Then find a way to bring it to life and put your personal stamp on it. It is the heart and personality we inject into our writing that makes it come alive.

It is the heart and personality we inject into our writing that makes it come alive.

35

Early Tips to Better Writing

Whether you have professional or creative goals for your writing, there are tips to create a smooth process.

Read great writers. You have probably heard this many times throughout this blog, but it is important. If you do not read strong writing, you won't know how to do it. Everyone starts by reading the masters. Read as much as possible. Pay attention to style, mechanics, and content.

Write often. Try to write every day – multiple times a day if your schedule allows it. Writing is a skill you can practice like playing a sport or learning a musical instrument. Write for different purposes. You can write for business, write for a blog, write for a publication, and more. Writing gets easier with practice.

Write down ideas, no matter how random. Keep a journal offline or on your mobile device. Throughout the day, jot down ideas from conversations, music, media, etc. Later you may find gems that inspire you to develop a novel character, a magazine article, or a story to introduce a PowerPoint presentation.

Create a writing ritual. Find a regular time each day to write. It may be for 15 minutes, 30 minutes, or more. If you can write for at least an hour, that is the best. Choose a good time of day. Maybe you're an early bird and do your best thinking in the morning? Maybe you're a night owl and prefer to write when others are sleeping? Do what works for you. Pick a routine you can commit to.

Writing is a skill you can practice like playing a sport or learning a musical instrument.

36
Early Tips to Better Writing – Part 2

The holiday season is upon us. This may be the hardest time of year to find time to write. But try anyway. Take time for yourself and the creative muse.

Clear away distractions. Turn off the television, turn off email, and turn off the cell phone. You might choose to play mellow music. Do not try to write and multi-task at the same time. It doesn't help your creativity!

Experiment with your writing. Yes, it is important to read master writers. But do not copy their style. You can borrow a few bits and pieces; however, you need to find your own style, voice, mechanics, themes, etc. See what works for you. Toss the rest.

Revising is key to becoming a better writer. In the beginning you should spill your guts in words. Spelling, grammar, and punctuation do not matter - just write until you cannot write anymore. But if you want to be a good writer, you must learn to revise. Check the mechanics. Also, go back over the writing and look for awkwardness, confusing, or unnecessary language.

Get feedback. Do not write in a vacuum. Find someone to read over your writing. If you have a friend with a writing or editing background, that's even better. Someone who reads often can also give great feedback. Be a good listener and accept the criticism. Learn from the feedback. Don't take anything personal.

Share your writing. After a certain point, you should share your work outside your circle of friends and family. Find a more public platform. You may decide to write for a publication. Maybe you'll post your writings online. Perhaps you will write a guest post for someone who is more established. Take the risk. Give it a try. Have a thick skin. See what happens when you share your writing with the world.

In the beginning you should spill your guts in words. Spelling, grammar, and punctuation do not matter - just write until you cannot write anymore.

37

How to Write a Holiday Thank You

"Gratitude turns what we have into enough." – Anon

Saying thank you is not limited by time or space. A kind gesture may be large, small, or even behind the scenes. At this time of year be diligent with saying thank you to family, friends, and coworkers.

Handwrite the thank you note. Do not just text! Also avoid sending an email or typed letter. A handwritten note is a more sincere way to express gratitude for a kindness.

Use nice stationary. If you are an arts and craft person, you can make it yourself or make it family time with kids. You may also choose to buy the stationary. Choose something that fits your style. There are options. You may decide on embossed or monogrammed stationary. Or something more casual from the local office supply store.

Personalize your message. If you expect to see the person soon, reference the event and your anticipation. If the person gave you an item you can use later, share how and when you plan to use it.

Better late than never. Even if you think it is too late to send a note, send it anyway. It's the thought that counts.

Use your best handwriting. You might want to practice your message on plain paper a few times. Then when you are ready, put your absolute best on the stationary.

Send a thanks, no matter how small. At this time of year, you never know what someone may be going through personally. Say thank you no matter how small the gesture. Say thank you often. There is no limit to experiencing and giving gratitude.

Saying thank you is not limited by time or space.

38

How to Journal Your Thoughts

In many parts of the world, it is time for the holidays. The year is ending, and we will soon roll into 2020. It can be a busy time. It can be a stressful time. Be careful about griping to other people who have their own lives to manage. **Write it down!**

Choose a journal that inspires you. Don't choose a journal that is so fancy and expensive that you don't want to write in it. Pick a reasonable size. If it is too big, you can't easily carry it around. If it is too small, your writing might be cramped or a strain to read. Choose a paper journal. With a paper journal you do not need to boot up, recharge, or download when you feel inspired to write.

Date your journal entry. When the time is right, you might decide to reread your thoughts. With a date, you can reflect on your evolution, grand adventures, or repeating cycles in your life.

Tell the truth….at least to yourself. In life we have different roles to play—husband, mother, sister, nephew, employee, friend, etc. At times, we might present a certain face to navigate the waters. In your journal, tell the truth. If you feel angry—say you are angry. If you feel sad—talk about why. If you feel like king of the mountain—brag and brag until your heart is content.

Write down the details of the situation or location. Use the five senses: sight, sound, touch, smell, hear, and taste.

Write a lot or write a little. No one is going to see the writing unless you choose to share. It's all about you. Write in prose, poetry, or even try a word collage. You decide.

Write a lot or write a little. No one is going to see the writing unless you choose to share.

39

How to Write a Song

Are you enjoying the holiday music on the radio, television, and gatherings with friends and family? Try your hand at songwriting. You don't have to be super serious and dream about winning a Grammy. **Songwriting can be a creative outlet to share with others**.

The first step is to use raw material for your lyrics. Choose a song title. Deliver the main message in your song through a concise title. Use six words or less.

Build questions around the song title. Who is your audience? What kind of questions might the audience ask? Brainstorm questions around the title. Think about the feelings and emotions the song might inspire. Develop a story or situation around the title. Focus on three to four big questions.

Choose a song structure. Popular songs we hear today have the following structure: Verse / Chorus / Verse / Chorus / Bridge / Chorus. Some songs have a section called a "lift" between the verse and chorus to build enthusiasm. Choose a melody to repeat throughout the song. The listeners will become familiar with the repeated melody.

Choose one question to answer in each chorus. Choose one question to answer in each verse. Respond in a short phrase. Tap into feelings and emotions. Use the five senses: sight, sound, touch, smell, hear, and taste.

Find the melody in your song. Practice the song out loud. Practice and tweak the song until it feels right, sounds right, and tells the story you want to tell.

Practice and tweak the song until it feels right, sounds right, and tells the story you want to tell.

40

How to Write Personal Objectives

Approximately half (50%) of all Americans make New Year's resolutions. Only 8% keep the resolution by the end of the year. Fitness and losing weight are the most common goals.

This year dare to be different. Write personal objectives for yourself using SMART goals. Achieve your dreams.

Be Specific. Choose an objective that is important to you around career, family, personal passions, etc. Write the objective down and explain why it is necessary.

Use a Measurable objective. You should be able to quantify or measure the objective in numbers. If you want to save a down payment for a house, what percentage of your salary do you need to save each month? If you want to write a 300-page novel, how many pages do you need to write each day? Clearly define the goal.

Choose an Achievable goal. You might need to do a little bit of research to select a measurable objective. If you choose a goal that is too high, you might feel discouraged by the end. If you choose a goal to low, you might not reach significant change in your circumstances.

Be Realistic. We may dream of being Superman and Wonder Woman, but we are mostly ordinary people. Choose personal goals that are realistic for you and your life. Consider your resources and personal skills. Will you need some training or education to reach your goal? If so, factor in the resources needed to evolve into a better you.

Set a Time limit. The personal objective must be time constrained. Setting a deadline will motivate you to get things done. Time limits also give a sense of urgency to avoid procrastinating.

We may dream of being Superman and Wonder Woman, but we are mostly ordinary people. Choose personal goals that are realistic for you and your life.

41

Happy New Year! Write that Resume – Part 1

January normally starts a hiring boom in multiple industries. Use this 4-part blog series to craft a resume that will land you the right job.

Make sure you understand resume basics before you start writing. You must condense your work experience into a concise, easy to read, typo-free document. Capitalize on relevant experiences, highlight measurable accomplishments, and add a dash of job skills.

Five Components of Every Resume

Contact Information. Your resume needs current contact information. Be sure to include the following: name, city and state, phone number, and email address. If you have a strictly professional social media page, include that as well. If you have a social media page that shows you enjoying cocktails on the beach, do not include it. As a matter of fact, clean up all social media profiles to avoid being prejudged by employers for your personal interests.

Resume Summary. After the contact information, you need a summary of your experience and best career highlights. It is almost as if you are showing the "coming attractions" in a movie starring you – the Best Employee Ever! Make the highlights relevant to the job. Use numbers to show measured success. Do not be shy about the great things you have done in previous positions.

Skills Section. The skills section should be below the summary. It should also use a short-bulleted format. The keywords should be a good match to the job you are applying for. Remember to also add soft skills such as problem-solving, communication, negotiation, etc.

Professional Experience. This is the main meal to your 5-course dinner! Do not make the mistake of just listing job duties. Focus on quantifiable accomplishments. How did you solve problems or save the company in your previous positions? Using numbers, dollars, and percentages will really make you shine.

Education. Do not make recruiters and hiring managers hunt for your education. Give it a separate section. If you are a new graduate, education goes at the top. If you have been in the workforce for several years, education goes at the bottom of the resume.

You must condense your work experience into a concise, easy to read, typo-free document (resume).

42

New Year, New You! Write that Resume – Part 2

Welcome to the second blog post in a four-part series on resume writing.

Employers only spend 10 seconds glancing at a resume. You need to grab their attention and pull them in with a great resume title. Do a little research to understand the appropriate job titles for your industry. However, you must make yourself look unique. Look at what has been done in the past, then punch it up with a few key words that make you stand out.

Choose a headline strategy. Your resume title should be concise. Consider using bold, italics, or capitalized letters. But remain conservative and professional. Avoid bright colors and font better suited for arts and crafts projects. If you have space for a sub-heading, this is the place to add your personal stamp. Refer to an accomplishment or skill that helped you rock it in a previous project or position. Also remember to tailor the headline to the industry you want to be in.

Use a career objective. Do not literally label the career objective as an "objective" in the resume. The content of your objective should be woven into your career summary. The objective should send the message of – *this is who I am as a professional, competent employee.* Avoid the giving the impression – *this is who I want to be in the future.* The objective should show your benefit to the company. Remember to be concise and specific.

The (resume) objective should show your benefit to the company. Remember to be concise and specific.

43
Write that Resume – Part 3, The Hook

Welcome to the third blog post in a four-part series on resume writing.

Hiring managers are busy people. A single job posting might attract hundreds if not thousands of resumes! Hiring managers are not reading every resume word for word. They scan for a career summary.

A career summary is a hard-hitting introduction packed with top notch skills, accomplishments, abilities, and attributes. Basically, this is how you stand out from the crowd.

Research your ideal job. It is important to tailor your summary to the job. Search for your ideal positions. Then, compile a list of common job requirements and preferred qualifications.

Assess your qualifications. How do you measure up? Be confident, but humble. You do not have to match every aspect of the job vacancy, 100%. But you do not want to land the job and require basic training on your day-to-day responsibilities. Outside of the minimum requirements, can you describe bonus skills you bring to the table? Also, if you are lacking in one area, how can you make up for in another area? Remember to clearly relay how you would benefit to the company.

Focus on your goal. Good career summaries target one career goal. If you have more than one career goal, consider drafting more than one version of your resume. Use bullets that will keep the resume easy to read.

Proofread, refine, and perfect. No matter how you tackle resume writing, you get one chance to make a first impression. Avoid simple errors.

Hiring managers are not reading every resume word for word. They scan for a career summary.

44

Write that Resume – Part 4, The Meat

Welcome to the last blog post in the 4-part series on resume writing in 2020.

Hiring Managers have a difficult task. They need to fill job vacancies, but they must wade through poorly written resumes. Help a prospective employer make a quick decision to call you by crafting a nice resume. The work history is the real "meat" to any resume.

There are several ways to punch things up and make you look like a winner. The right resume will get the interview.

Do not copy the job description. Some job seekers copy and paste the job description. Big no-no! Emphasize your accomplishments in previous positions. Quantify it. Use numbers, dollars, and percentages. Highlight how you saved the company.

Boast your problem-solving skills. Describe challenges, actions to overcome challenges, and results of your efforts in your work experience. Before you write the work history, you might consider drafting a list of all accomplishments in the last 10 years. Add the most impressive accomplishments to the resume. Write the result of your efforts, before concisely describing the problem and action.

Make it readable. Use a combination of bullets and paragraphs in work histories to keep it readable but not monotonous. Hiring managers need to be able to rest their eyes. Clearly label accomplishments as "accomplishments" or "key contributions." Be concise. The resume should hook the reader and land you an interview. Do not tell your whole life story in a resume.

As always target the job vacancy. Use power words. You can find powerful verbs and synonyms online. Be honest. An honest and well-written resume will be called for interviews.

Have another person proofread your resume. When we write and read our own work it can be hard to catch mistakes. Before sending your resume to prospective employers, have a trusted person read over the resume. Have a friend proofread and check for tone.

Help a prospective employer make a quick decision to call you by crafting a nice resume.

45

How to Write a Cover Letter – Dip a Toe into the Pool

Welcome to this five-part series on writing cover letters.

Ack. Job hunting. Nobody likes it. Unless you have family or friends to make connections for you, you are fighting an uphill battle. The best thing you can do is arm yourself with knowledge. Knowledge is power.

We live in a digital age. Some may wonder if we still need cover letters. Not sending a cover letter, makes you look a little lazy. If a hiring manager has two equal resumes side by side, the resume with the cover letter will get the interview call.

Before you start writing, do your research. Research the company and the specific job that you want. Review the company's website, twitter feeds, and executive profiles on LinkedIn. Try to read beyond the job description. If you know the company's challenges, you can write a cover letter describing yourself as the solution. The research will also help you determine the tone of your letter. Are you writing to appeal to risk-taking creative company? Or are you trying to appeal to an ultra-conservative organization, like a bank?

The next step to take after researching the company, is to open strong. Typically, people churn out the usual, "I am applying to job Z that I saw on website X." Don't do this! Jump in with enthusiasm. Tell the hiring manager why the job is exciting to you and why you're the right fit. The hiring lead is probably reading mountains of resumes. You need to stand out. Be direct. Be dynamic. But don't tell any jokes. Humor can fall flat.

If you have a personal connection with the company or someone who works there, mention this in the first line or two. Always direct your letter to someone by name. With social media, you can find the name of the hiring manager.

Try to read beyond the job description. If you know the company's challenges, you can write a cover letter describing yourself as the solution.

46

How to Write a Cover Letter – Shining with Pizazz!

Welcome to part two of a five-part series on writing cover letters.

Hiring managers are looking for candidates that can help them solve problems. Building on the company research you conducted in step one of cover letter writing, you should know the company's biggest hurdles. You don't have to be too detailed but address a challenging trend in the industry in your cover letter.

Give an example of an industry challenge. Then talk about your experience that has equipped you to meet the challenge. Describe a situation where you solved a similar problem in another position. Highlight relevant accomplishments.

Show enthusiasm. Be clear about why you want the position. Today's job market has a lot of job seekers with different skill sets. Show your passion for the position. You really shouldn't apply to any job that doesn't inspire your enthusiasm or build excitement.

Sending out 200 resumes is a waste of time. Pick 6-10 companies you really want to work for and put some muscle into your applications. Be authentic. Do not go overboard with flattery or fudge the truth. No matter your age or stage in life, be mature and professional. Tailor the cover letter to the company and only use language the hiring manage would use.

Be concise. Do not tell your whole life story in a cover letter. The letter should be under one page. Shorter is better.

Be concise. Do not tell your whole life story in a cover letter.

47

How to Write a Cover Letter – Avoid Common Pitfalls

Welcome to part three of the five-part series on writing cover letters.

In this blog post, we are going to discuss how you can avoid common pitfalls in cover letters. Many job seekers repeat their resume in the cover letter, word for word. Do not do this! Pick 3-4 relevant accomplishments in your resume and use the cover letter to BRAG. Do not be afraid to brag about your work experiences. Just be concise and honest.

When you dig deeper into your accomplishments in the cover letter, describe your approach to problem solving. Talk as if you are giving story details to a new friend but communicate in bullets. Highlight the personality, passion, and work ethic that helped you be a hero for your last company.

Another common pitfall in writing a cover letter is not fully describing what you bring to the table. Clearly define the ways you can be of service to the company. Demonstrate how you are the right person to solve the company problems. Do not talk about how great the position would be for you personally.

In the cover letter, highlight the right experiences for the position. The most important job requirements are typically listed first in the job description or mentioned more than once. Make sure you describe how you can deliver on those key priorities.

Lastly, do not apologize for missing experience. Job hunting can test our confidence and determination. If you feel inadequate in any way about the position, do not mention it. Never draw attention to your weaknesses. You do not have to have 100% of the qualifications to be hired in today's job market. Play to your strengths.

You do not have to have 100% of the qualifications to be hired in today's job market. Play to your strengths.

48

Spring Forward, Spring into That New Job!

Hiring managers are looking for candidates that can help them solve problems. Building on the company research you conducted in step one of cover letter writing, you should know the company's biggest hurdles. You don't have to be too detailed but address a challenging trend in the industry in your cover letter.

Give an example of an industry challenge. Then talk about your experience that has equipped you to meet the challenge. Describe a situation where you solved a similar problem in another position. Highlight relevant accomplishments…

Many job seekers repeat their resume in the cover letter, word for word. Don't do this! Pick 3-4 relevant accomplishments in your resume and use the cover letter to BRAG. Do not be afraid to brag about your work experiences. Just be concise and honest.

When you dig deeper into your accomplishments in the cover letter, describe your approach to problem solving. Talk as if you are giving story details to a new friend but communicate in bullets. Highlight the personality, passion, and work ethic that helped you be a hero for your last company.

Highlight the personality, passion, and work ethic that helped you be a hero for your last company.

49

How to Write a Cover Letter – Getting Creative!

Today's job market is competitive. If you don't have an inside connection with the hiring company, you really need to cross your t's and dot your i's.

Welcome to the fourth installation in the five-part series on writing cover letters.

Hiring managers love to see statistics. Quantify work experience in the cover letter. Use numbers to describe measurable success in other positions. Did you save the company revenue? Did you save the company on product delivery? How many new clients did you recruit? Even if previous positions centered around soft skills and managing people, you can find creative ways to use numbers and stand out. Learn more here:

Consider testimonials. Do you have good quotes from managers in your performance evaluation? Have clients or co-workers mentioned you or your project in social media? Use written feedback from different platforms to add *star power* to your cover letters.

Write the cover letter in the company's voice. As mentioned in earlier blog posts, research the company through their website and social media to understand their culture. Use your findings to draft a cover letter in the appropriate tone and language.

Remember to show enthusiasm but don't spell out that you are excited. And watch the adverbs! Some candidates may write, "I am super excited to apply for job Z!" No, don't do this. Yes, show your personality, creativity, and excitement. Write like a normal person. Use a thesaurus every now and then.

Hiring managers love to see statistics. Quantify work experience in the cover letter.

50

How to Write a Cover Letter – Bringing Home the Bacon

As the world spins around us with uncertainty, use the time at home to develop yourself professionally. When the chaos clears, you will be ready to step up and step out.

Welcome to the fifth and final installation in the series on writing cover letters. We're almost there. Put the finishing touches on your cover letter.

Keep it short and sweet. Most hiring managers like a cover page that is under one page. Half a page is even better. If you're a numbers person, aim for 250-300 words.

End the cover letter on a strong note. Don't do the generic, "I look forward to speaking with you." Rock it! Add an important detail such as being willing to relocate.

Edit, edit, edit. Of course, we all know to spell check by now. But really, double check, and triple check the spelling. Read beyond the computer-generated spell check. Set the cover letter aside for about 24 hours, more if you can spare the time. Then come back with a fresh pair of eyes. Consider free online services that check grammar. Enlist the help of family or friends. You only get *one* chance to make a first impression.

As the world spins around us with uncertainty, use the time at home to develop yourself professionally.

Thank You for Reading!

www.ingramcontent.com/pod-product-compliance
Lightning Source LLC
LaVergne TN
LVHW051526070426
835507LV00023B/3327